D1514529

City of Kings & Queens

The history of London stretches back more than two thousand years. For a thousand years it has been the home of kings and queens, who built palaces and churches throughout the city. Some of these, with their traditional royal ceremonies, survive today.

ROMAN LONDON

The Romans built the first city of London, and the first bridge across the River Thames, nearly two thousand years ago. They named their city Londinium and filled it with houses and temples. Trading ships carrying goods came from all over the Roman world.

A QUEEN ATTACKS

In the year 60, Queen Boudicca of the nearby Iceni people led an army to attack and destroy much of the city. The Romans rebuilt it and stayed for the next 400 years.

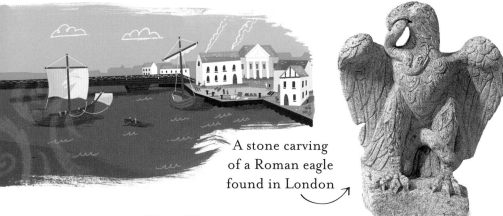

A stone carving of a Roman eagle found in London

THE KING MOVES IN

The first king to make his permanent home in London was Edward the Confessor. He built an abbey at Westminster, west of the Roman city. Completed in 1065, he died the next year and was buried there. You can still see his tomb today.

THE NORMANS ARRIVE

In 1066, Duke William of Normandy, known as William the Conqueror, invaded from France. He conquered England and made London his headquarters.

This 15th-century painting shows Edward the Confessor at a banquet.

This scene from the Bayeux Tapestry shows the arrival of the Normans on the English coast.

TUDOR LONDON

The kings and queens of the Tudor dynasty (1485-1603) loved building palaces. You can still see some, including St. James's and Hampton Court, today.

This painting shows Elizabeth I, the last Tudor monarch, being carried through the streets of London.

THE GREAT FIRE

In 1666, a fire started in a bakery and spread across much of London, destroying most of the medieval city. But a new city of magnificent stone buildings was soon planned to replace it.

The old St. Paul's Cathedral was destroyed and a new one was built in the same place.

VICTORIAN LONDON

During the reign of Queen Victoria (1837-1901), London grew into one of the largest and richest cities in the world.

One of the most splendid buildings to survive from Victorian London is the Albert Memorial. It was erected in Kensington Gardens in memory of Queen Victoria's husband, Prince Albert, following his death in 1861. A gold statue of the prince sits under a brightly patterned and carved stone canopy.

ROYAL LONDON TODAY

Many of the royal buildings erected over the centuries have been pulled down or destroyed in fires. But others still remain as working royal residences. Some, including Buckingham Palace and Hampton Court, are open to the public and they're visited by thousands of people from all over the world.

Tower of London

William the Conqueror began building the Tower of London more than 900 years ago. It was designed both as a royal palace and a fort from where he could keep a close eye on any troublesome citizens. Over the years, it has also been used as a prison and even a zoo.

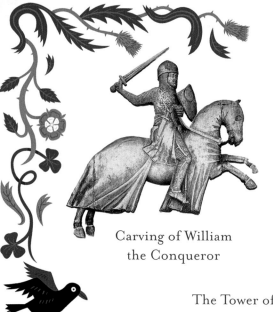

Carving of William the Conqueror

A FORTRESS PALACE

The Tower of London is made up of a collection of buildings surrounding the original White Tower. It is one of the most popular sites visited by tourists.

In 2014, a display of red ceramic poppies represented all British and Colonial soldiers killed in the First World War.

Jewel House

Royal Chapel

Byward Tower

Tower Green

Moat

Traitor's Gate

GUARDIANS OF THE TOWER

The Yeomen Warders, also known as Beefeaters, have been guarding the Tower since the 1500s. Ravens have been kept at the Tower since the reign of King Charles II.

Legend tells that if the ravens ever leave, then the Tower, and England, will fall.

The ravens have their wings clipped to prevent them flying away. They are fed every day on fresh fruit, cheese and raw meat.

PRINCES IN THE TOWER

Two famous prisoners were the young sons of Edward IV, Princes Edward and Richard. In 1483, on the orders of their uncle Richard III, they were taken to the Tower. They were never seen again.

Princes Edward and Richard in the Tower, painted in 1830 by French artist Paul Delaroche.

THREE QUEENS

Throughout the 1500s, the Tower became a place of execution for some of England's most famous figures. Three queens - Anne Boleyn, Catherine Howard and Lady Jane Grey - were all beheaded on Tower Green inside the walls.

DID YOU KNOW?

Many of the prisoners were brought to the Tower by boat, and entered through a gate known as Traitor's Gate. Passing under London Bridge, they would have seen the severed heads of recently executed prisoners.

This scene of Lady Jane Grey's last moments was painted in 1833 by Paul Delaroche.

A ROYAL MENAGERIE

From 1210, during the reign of King John, the Tower was also used as a zoo. Animals including lions and monkeys were kept there. But after a number of attacks on visitors, they were moved to London Zoo in 1832.

Some dangerous animals attacked each other.

Crown Jewels

Inside the Tower of London, you can visit the Crown Jewels, a collection of some of the most famous and valuable jewels in the world. Dating back hundreds of years, they include crowns and other jewelled objects used in royal coronation ceremonies.

ST. EDWARD'S CROWN

The most important piece in the collection is St. Edward's Crown. Over 300 years old, it is made of solid gold and studded with precious stones, and used in the crowning of every new king or queen.

Queen Elizabeth II wears
St. Edward's Crown.

STUCK IN THE MUD

King John, who ruled England from 1199 until 1216, lost his crown and other jewels on a journey through Lincolnshire. The heavy carts laden with his gold and jewels sank into the muddy ground and disappeared. People have been searching for them ever since, but they've never been found.

This painting shows King John
out hunting, a favourite pastime.

SELLING OFF THE JEWELS

Most of the Crown Jewels date from 1661. Twelve years earlier, in 1649, King Charles I was executed and the old Crown Jewels were sold off by Parliament. So when his son, King Charles II, was restored to the throne, a new set was made for his coronation the following year.

Charles I

Charles II

IMPERIAL STATE CROWN

The Imperial State Crown is worn after the crowning ceremony and at every State Opening of Parliament. It is encrusted with more than 3,000 diamonds and other precious stones.

There is a huge sapphire at the back of the crown, known as the Stuart Sapphire. It once belonged to the kings of Scotland.

Four large pear-shaped pearls hang below the central cross. They were once worn as earrings by Elizabeth I.

St. Edward's Sapphire is set in the cross at the top. It once formed part of the coronation ring of Edward the Confessor, crowned King of England in 1043.

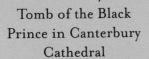

This painting shows Edward holding a ring.

The Black Prince's Ruby sits in the middle. It was given in 1367 to the son of Edward III, known as the Black Prince, by Pedro the Cruel, King of Castile in Spain.

An enormous diamond, known as Cullinan II and cut from the biggest diamond ever found, is set at the front of the crown.

Tomb of the Black Prince in Canterbury Cathedral

Queen Elizabeth I dressed in pearls

A RIGHT ROYAL ROBBERY

A daring robbery took place in 1671 when Colonel Thomas Blood broke into the Tower and made off with the royal jewels. He was caught, but King Charles II was so impressed by his audacity that he pardoned him, and even granted him a pension.

Westminster Abbey

Westminster Abbey is one of the most magnificent of all royal buildings in London, the scene of the coronations of kings and queens ever since 1066.

TOMBS OF FAMOUS PEOPLE

The Abbey is dedicated to St. Peter. At its heart lies the shrine of King Edward the Confessor. It is also the resting place of 16 other monarchs and contains hundreds of monuments to famous people, from poets and artists to statesmen and soldiers.

This scene from the Bayeux Tapestry shows the burial of Edward the Confessor.

Elizabeth I   Mary, Queen of Scots

RIVAL QUEENS

The tombs of Queen Elizabeth I and Mary, Queen of Scots lie close to each other. Although deadly rivals, they never met. Mary's body was moved to the Abbey by her son after he became King James I of England in 1603.

DID YOU KNOW?

In the 7th century, a fisherman called Aldrich saw a vision of St. Peter on the riverbank nearby. Today, every year, the Fishmonger's Company presents a gift of a salmon to the Abbey.

The North Entrance

A church has stood here since the 7th century. Henry III started the present building in 1245, and work continued over the next 500 years.

Lady Chapel

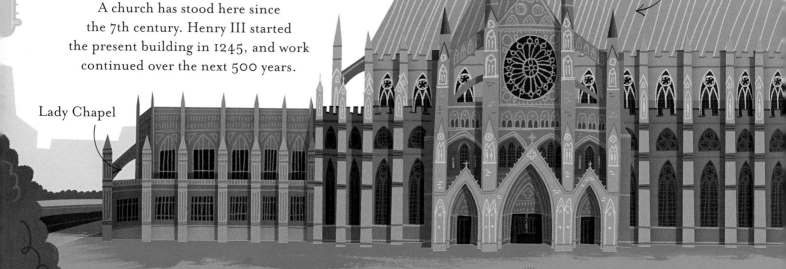

A LONG CEREMONY

Queen Victoria's coronation in 1838 was so long and tiring, that when they weren't needed, the royal party retreated to a side chapel where they could eat sandwiches and drink wine.

Stone ceiling with fan decoration

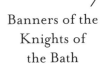

THE CORONATION CHAIR

Every monarch is crowned on the Coronation Chair. A space underneath holds a block of stone called the Stone of Scone. This ancient stone was used in the coronation of the monarchs of Scotland before unification.

THE LADY CHAPEL

King Henry VII, the first of the Tudor monarchs, built the beautiful Lady Chapel. He is buried there with his wife, Elizabeth of York, beneath a magnificent fan-vaulted ceiling, which you can see on the right.

Banners of the Knights of the Bath

Two towers were added between 1722 and 1745.

The Abbey has often been used for royal weddings and funerals too. In 2011, the Duke and Duchess of Cambridge were married here.

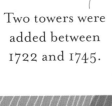

Palace of Westminster

The Palace of Westminster, known as the Houses of Parliament, is one of the most important buildings in Britain. Once the site of a royal palace built in about 1050, it is now home to the British Parliament which sits in the Houses of Lords and Commons.

THE FIRST PARLIAMENT

In 1295, Edward I summoned England's first official Parliament - known as the Model Parliament - which met in Westminster Hall, built on the north side of the palace. Parliament has met at the palace ever since.

This 16th-century painting shows Edward I presiding over a meeting of his Parliament.

DESTROYED BY FIRE

Although it was built as a palace, no monarch has lived here for hundreds of years. It has had a very turbulent history.
In 1605, Guy Fawkes tried to blow up the building when James I and his ministers were inside.
In 1834, most of the medieval palace was destroyed by fire.

A NEW PALACE

A new Palace of Westminster was completed in 1868, designed by an architect named Charles Barry. Inside, there are about 1,100 rooms, connected by 5km (3 miles) of corridors and 100 staircases. When the Union Flag flies on the Victoria Tower, this shows that Members of Parliament are meeting inside.

Victoria Tower

This carved stone detail from the exterior shows the royal coat of arms.

FIT FOR A QUEEN

Many of the interior fittings, from the golden thrones in the House of Lords to the painted ceilings and patterned floor tiles, were designed by another architect, named Augustus Pugin.

Golden throne with royal coat of arms

One of the many designs for floor tiles inside

ROYAL CHAPEL

The Chapel of Saint Mary Undercroft lies in the heart of the building. Completed by Edward III in about 1365, it was once used by his courtiers, and it is still a royal chapel.

This 14th-century painting shows the coronation of Edward III in 1327.

WESTMINSTER HALL

The oldest surviving part of the palace is Westminster Hall, built in 1097. Many important ceremonies take place here. For example, after their deaths, the bodies of kings and queens are brought here to 'lie in state' before their funerals.

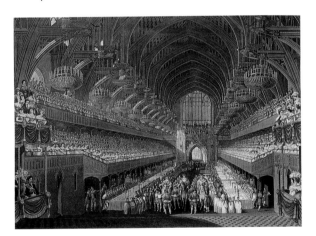

BIG BEN

Big Ben is the nickname of the largest of the five bells inside the clock tower. It may have been named after Benjamin Hall, who was in charge of the rebuilding of the Houses of Parliament.

The House of Lords and the House of Commons are in the central block.

A State Opening

Every year, in either May or June, the Queen comes to the Palace of Westminster to open a new session of Parliament. She plays the central part in the magnificent ceremony, which is known as the State Opening of Parliament.

THE ROYAL PROCESSION

The Queen travels in a carriage procession from Buckingham Palace to the Houses of Parliament. Her route takes her down the Mall, across Horse Guards (see page 17) and on to Westminster. A military band marches at the front of the royal procession.

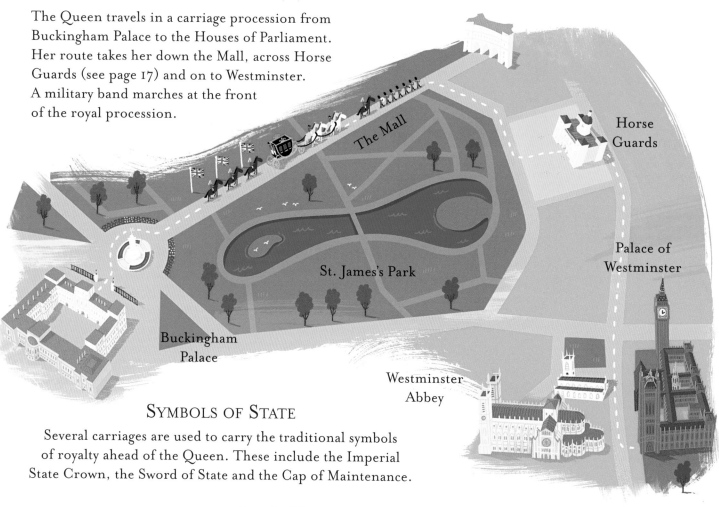

Horse Guards

The Mall

St. James's Park

Palace of Westminster

Buckingham Palace

Westminster Abbey

SYMBOLS OF STATE

Several carriages are used to carry the traditional symbols of royalty ahead of the Queen. These include the Imperial State Crown, the Sword of State and the Cap of Maintenance.

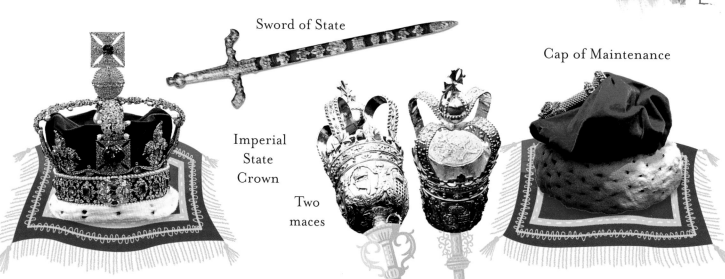

Sword of State

Cap of Maintenance

Imperial State Crown

Two maces

PLEASE OPEN THE DOOR!

A royal official known as 'Black Rod', because of the black staff he carries, is sent to summon the Members of Parliament from the House of Commons. As a symbol of their independence from the monarchy, the door to their chamber is slammed in his face. It is only opened when he has knocked on the door three times.

THE QUEEN'S SPEECH

Members of both Houses of Parliament and guests including judges and ambassadors gather in the House of Lords to listen to the Queen. She reads a speech describing what her government is planning for the year.

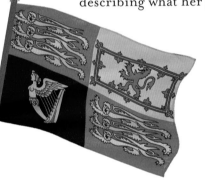

The Union Flag which flies on top of the Victoria Tower is replaced by the Royal Standard - the Queen's personal flag - to show that she is present.

A ROYAL HOSTAGE

During the ceremony, a Member of Parliament (MP) is 'held hostage' at Buckingham Palace, and is only released when the Queen is safely back home.

SEARCHING THE CELLARS

On the morning of every State Opening, the Yeomen of the Guard - Her Majesty's bodyguards - search the cellars beneath the Houses of Parliament. This has been done ever since 1605, when Guy Fawkes and accomplices tried to blow up King James I and his ministers.

This tradition dates to the power struggle between the King and Parliament during the reign of Charles I. The 'hostage' is very well looked after while at the palace.

James I

St. James's

The royal palace of St. James gave its name to an area in the heart of London. Other royal residences were built nearby, and shops opened to supply the royal court with clothes, food, wines and luxury goods.

A TUDOR PALACE

St. James's Palace was completed in 1536 for King Henry VIII on the site of a hospital dedicated to Saint James the Less, one of the twelve Apostles of Christ. It is the oldest surviving London palace, although much of it was destroyed by fire in 1809. The official title of foreign ambassadors to Britain is 'Ambassador to the Court of St. James'.

The impressive Tudor gateway into St. James's Palace

WARMING PAN BABY

The baby son of Catholic James II and his second wife, Mary of Modena, was born at St. James's Palace in 1688. But many Protestants feared a revival of Catholic influence in the country. Rumours spread that the baby wasn't the King's child at all, and had been smuggled into the royal apartments in a bed warming pan.

James II

You can often see soldiers in their furry bearskin hats on either side of the gateway.

THE QUEEN'S CHAPEL

One of the most elegant buildings in St. James's is the Queen's Chapel. This was designed by Inigo Jones and completed in 1627 for Charles I's wife, Henrietta Maria. When the palace's royal apartments were destroyed in the 1809 fire, the chapel was left standing alone.

BY ROYAL APPOINTMENT

Many of the shops that sprang up around the royal court survive today. Berry Brothers have been selling wine in St. James's Street since 1698, and grocery store Fortnum & Mason opened in 1707. Other shops in the area that have been around for centuries include Paxton & Whitfield (cheeses), Floris (scents) and Locks (hatters).

This fancy clock hangs above the main entrance to Fortnum & Mason in Piccadilly.

Shop sign of wine merchants Berry Brothers

Queen Henrietta Maria

ST. JAMES'S PARK

St. James's Park is one of the smallest and oldest of the London royal parks, founded by James I. A nearby road called Pall Mall is named after *paille maille*, a form of croquet Charles II used to play in the park.

This early 18th-century painting shows cows grazing in the park, on the right.

Charles II kept wild animals in the park, including an elephant. The area where he kept exotic birds is still known as Birdcage Walk.

Whitehall

Whitehall gets its name from the huge, rambling Palace of Whitehall, which was the main royal residence in London from 1530 until it burned down in 1698. Today, it's where many government offices are located.

A ROYAL SMASH AND GRAB

The palace was named after the white stone that was used to build it. Originally the London residence of Cardinal Wolsey, Archbishop of York, it was snatched by Henry VIII when the cardinal fell from power.

This 17th-century painting shows the buildings of Whitehall Palace. The Banqueting House is on the left.

Wolsey was Henry VIII's chief minister and for a time the most powerful person in the land.

BANQUETING HOUSE

The only part of the palace to survive the fire is the Banqueting House, designed by famous architect Inigo Jones for James I and completed in 1622. His son, Charles I, commissioned a magnificent painting in honour of his father to decorate the ceiling.

Painted by famous artist Peter Paul Rubens, this is one of the most splendid painted ceilings in the whole of Europe.

THE KING'S EXECUTION

Charles I fought a Civil War with his Parliament during the 1640s. He was defeated and sentenced to death. The Banqueting House had been one of his favourite buildings, and in 1649 he was executed on a scaffold erected in front of it.

The execution was in winter, and Charles wore two shirts so he didn't give the impression he was shivering in fear.

Charles I

REMEMBRANCE DAY

The Cenotaph was erected after the First World War, to commemorate the British servicemen and women who died in the War and all the wars since. Every year, the Queen and other members of the Royal Family attend a Remembrance Day service there.

HORSE GUARDS

Horse Guards is where the royal stables used to be. The present building, completed in 1753, is the headquarters of the Household Cavalry, part of the Queen's official bodyguard. Every June, the Queen's Birthday Parade, known as Trooping the Colour, is held at Horse Guards.

A cavalry soldier at the Queen's Birthday Parade. The design of his uniform dates back 200 years.

Badge of the Household Cavalry. The motto, from the royal coat of arms, means "Shame be to him who thinks evil of it".

Greenwich

Greenwich has been associated with royalty ever since 1427, when Duke Humphrey of Gloucester built himself a house there beside the River Thames. King Henry VI and his new bride Margaret of Anjou loved the area so much that they built a new palace, naming it Placentia or the 'Pleasant Place'.

Royal Naval Hospital

The Queen's House

The Royal Observatory

THE QUEEN'S HOUSE

King James I gave the palace to his wife, Anne, daughter of King Frederick II of Denmark. She commissioned a new, smaller home for herself, now named the Queen's House after her.

Queen Anne

Part of a painted ceiling in the Queen's House

ROYAL NAVAL HOSPITAL

Mary II, Queen Anne's great-granddaughter and wife of King William III, had the old palace pulled down at the end of the 17th century. It was rebuilt as a hospital for wounded sailors, designed by Christopher Wren and Nicholas Hawksmoor.

Sea lion badge of the Naval Hospital

Queen Mary's one request was that the new building should not interrupt the views to the river from the Queen's House.

THE PAINTED HALL

One wing of the Hospital contains a huge painted hall, covered by the largest painted ceiling in Britain. It took the artist, James Thornhill, 20 years to complete, and shows William and Mary floating up into the clouds and spreading peace across Europe.

Mary II

QUEEN'S CHAPEL

In the other wing of the Hospital is the Queen's Chapel, damaged by fire and rebuilt in the early 18th century.

ROYAL OBSERVATORY

The Royal Observatory, established during the reign of Charles II and designed by Christopher Wren, was the first purpose-built scientific building in the country. It is now a museum open to the public and contains a world-famous collection of scientific instruments.

John Harrison's first marine clock which can be seen in the museum

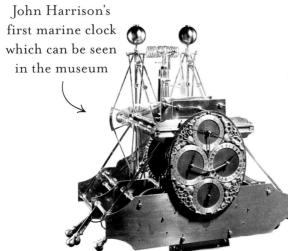

A ROYAL DEER PARK

Greenwich Park is the oldest enclosed royal park in London. Henry VIII first introduced deer in the park 500 years ago and liked to go hunting there. It is situated on a hilltop with magnificent views over the River Thames.

St. Paul's Cathedral

St. Paul's Cathedral is one of London's most famous royal buildings. Its great dome is one of the biggest in the world, and you can climb up 528 steps to the very top. For 300 years after its completion, the Cathedral was the tallest building in London.

This golden figure of St. Paul can be seen inside.

The south-west tower contains a huge bell, called the Great Paul.

The Cathedral is built of Portland stone from Dorset.

A statue of Queen Anne, the reigning monarch when the building was completed in 1710, stands in front.

A NEW CATHEDRAL

There has been a church on this site dedicated to St. Paul ever since the year 604. The present building, dating to the late 17th century, replaced a medieval cathedral that was destroyed in the Great Fire of London of 1666.

A BEACON OF HOPE

In the Second World War, the Cathedral became a symbol of defiance and hope when bombs were falling during the Blitz. Although it was hit, the Prime Minister Winston Churchill ordered that St. Paul's be saved for the morale of the country.

This photograph shows St. Paul's during the Blitz.

DID YOU KNOW?

The architect of St. Paul's, Christopher Wren, is buried inside. The Cathedral contains the tombs of many other famous people, including those of Admiral Lord Nelson and the Duke of Wellington.

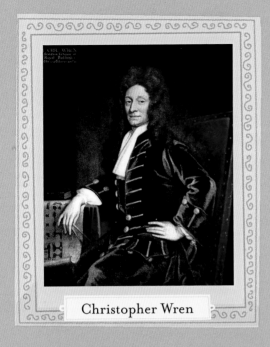

Christopher Wren

This view towards the High Altar shows the elaborately patterned ceilings above.

The Cathedral ceiling is decorated with brightly patterned mosaics.

Mosaic angels above the Altar

ROYAL WEDDING

The Prince of Wales and Lady Diana Spencer were married at the Cathedral in 1981. Hundreds of thousands of cheering well-wishers lined the streets, and the service was watched by more than 750 million people all over the world.

DIAMOND JUBILEES

Two great British queens celebrated their Diamond Jubilees - 60-year reigns - at St. Paul's. Queen Victoria held hers in June 1897, and 115 years later, her great-great-granddaughter, Elizabeth II, celebrated hers in June 2012.

The Prince and Princess of Wales leave St. Paul's after their wedding.

Royal Hospital Chelsea

One of the grandest royal buildings in London isn't a palace at all, but a retirement home for old soldiers. King Charles II laid the foundation stone for the Royal Hospital in 1682. Designed by Christopher Wren, it was completed 10 years later in the reign of William III.

Charles II

INSIDE THE HOSPITAL

The residents of the Royal Hospital are known as Chelsea Pensioners. They're famous for their uniforms of scarlet jackets and black hats. On one side of the building is the Chapel, and on the other side is the Great Hall where the Pensioners take their meals.

Painting of Christ in the Chapel

Charles II in the Great Hall

THE CHELSEA PENSIONERS

The first Pensioners were veterans of the English Civil War fought between Charles I and Parliament during the 1640s. The painting on the left shows one of the Civil War battles. Until 2009, Pensioners were all retired male soldiers. But retired women soldiers are admitted now too.

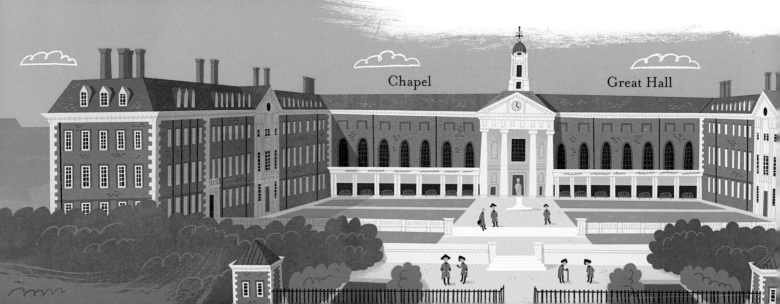

Chapel

Great Hall

FOUNDER'S DAY

Founder's Day, held on May 29, celebrates Charles II's birthday, and his restoration to the throne in 1660. Pensioners wear oak leaves in memory of the time when the King hid from Parliamentary soldiers in an oak tree.

A PERSUASIVE MISTRESS

According to legend, King Charles was persuaded to build the hospital by his favourite mistress, Nell Gwyn. Her own father had fought in the Civil War and had been ruined by it.

Nell Gwyn

THE CHELSEA FLOWER SHOW

Since 1913, the grounds of the Royal Hospital have been the grand setting for the Royal Horticultural Society's Chelsea Flower Show. It is held over five days every May. The Queen comes to visit with other members of the Royal Family.

A GOLDEN STATUE

A golden statue of Charles II stands outside the Hospital. Made by an artist named Grinling Gibbons in the late 17th century, it was regilded for the Queen's Golden Jubilee in 2002.

On Founder's Day, King Charles's statue is decorated with garlands of oak leaves.

William III

Mary II

Kensington Palace

Kensington Palace, in west London, was a private house until 1689, when it was bought by William III and his wife Mary II as a refuge from the polluted air of the city. It was enlarged during the 18th century when it was the home of several kings and queens.

A GRACEFUL DESCENT

The next monarch was Mary's sister, Anne, who commissioned the famous architect Christopher Wren to add another wing. This contained a staircase with shallow steps, specially designed to enable the portly queen to walk up and down gracefully.

PALACE PETS

The next king, George I, kept Bengal tigers at the palace. But they were so fierce that their keeper demanded danger money!

BY INVITATION ONLY

During the 18th century, the formal gardens surrounding Kensington Palace became so famous that they were occasionally opened to the public - but only to those who were respectably dressed.

People who weren't allowed to enter the gardens used to stand outside the gates, loudly mocking the lucky ones inside.

BIRTHPLACE OF A QUEEN

Princess Victoria, granddaughter of George III, was born at
Kensington Palace and brought up there by her widowed mother.
It was there in 1837, at the age of 18, that she heard that her uncle,
William IV, had died and that she was now the new queen.

The marble statue of Queen Victoria outside
the palace was made by her daughter, Princess
Louise, a gifted sculptor who had a studio there.

This portrait shows the young
Princess Victoria with her
mother, the Duchess of Kent.

A PLACE OF MOURNING

In August 1997, Kensington Palace became the focus of worldwide
mourning at the death of Diana, Princess of Wales, who had lived there
since her marriage in 1981. Thousands of people from all over
the world came to leave flowers and pay their respects.

THE PALACE TODAY

Kensington Palace is still home to many members
of the Royal Family. The Duke of Cambridge, heir
to the throne, was brought up at the palace, and he
and his wife now live there with their young children,
Prince George and Princess Charlotte.

Buckingham Palace

Buckingham Palace is the Queen's official London residence. It's where great state occasions take place, such as banquets for visiting heads of state, and it's the focus of national celebrations, such as the Queen's Diamond Jubilee in 2012.

FROM TOWN HOUSE TO PALACE

The palace was originally the residence of the Duke of Buckingham. Then in 1761, George III bought it for his wife, Queen Charlotte. It was enlarged by their son, George IV, but Queen Victoria was the first reigning monarch to live there, moving in when she became Queen in 1837.

This view of Buckingham Palace shows what it looked like in 1840, soon after Victoria moved in.

DID YOU KNOW?

The palace used to have an open courtyard in front. But Queen Victoria felt too exposed to public view, so in 1850 she had a marble gateway moved and a new east wing built across the front.

The gateway was taken down and moved to its present position near Oxford Street, where it's known as Marble Arch.

This memorial to Queen Victoria was erected outside Buckingham Palace in 1911.

PALACE OF TREASURES

The palace is full of spectacular treasures - priceless paintings, furniture, porcelain, gold and silver. They are part of the Royal Collection, one of the most famous and valuable art collections in the world.

This gold tiger's head was part of an Indian throne.

TEA IN THE GARDENS

Behind the palace is the largest private garden in London, covering 17 hectares (42 acres). The Queen holds garden parties there every summer and the specially invited guests drink tea and eat sandwiches while a band plays.

QUEEN'S GALLERY

During the Second World War, a bomb destroyed the palace chapel.

As well as immaculate lawns, flower beds and trees, there is a lake with a flock of flamingos, a tennis court and helicopter landing pad.

This picture shows George VI and Queen Elizabeth inspecting the damage. It was rebuilt and is now the Queen's Gallery where you can see works of art from the Royal Collection.

THE ROYAL MEWS

You can also visit the Royal Mews, where the Queen's magnificent state coaches and official cars are kept, as well as about 30 horses.

Hampton Court

Hampton Court is an enormous brick and stone palace beside the Thames to the west of London. It began as a residence for Henry VIII's chief minister, Cardinal Wolsey. But the king cast his greedy eyes over it, so the cardinal thought it wise to present it to his master. This didn't help Wolsey, however, as he was sacked soon after.

FOOD FOR THE COURT

When Henry VIII and his court were in residence, the palace kitchens had to provide food for about one thousand people every day. So Henry added huge new kitchens. Today, you can often see demonstrations of Tudor cooking in the kitchens.

CHAPEL ROYAL

Henry also redesigned the Chapel, giving it one of the most richly decorated ceilings in the country. It's believed to be haunted by the ghost of Catherine Howard, Henry's fifth wife, who was dragged screaming from here to her execution in the Tower of London.

Kitchens and servants' quarters

HENRY'S CROWN

There's a modern copy of a gold crown set with jewels in the chapel. The original was worn by Henry VIII and his three children - Edward VI, Mary I and Elizabeth I.

SOME EXTRA ROOMS

In the late 1600s, Hampton Court became a popular residence of William III and Mary II. They commissioned Christopher Wren to add new wings, doubling the size of the palace and turning it into the huge building it is today.

In 1540, Henry had an elaborate astronomical clock fitted outside.

William and Mary added new wings at the back of the palace.

Wolsey's original palace has groups of ornately patterned brick chimneys on the roof.

Sculptures of fantastical stone beasts decorate the main entrance.

Great Hall

Main entrance

Fences with delicate wrought iron screens border the River Thames, so that people inside the palace could see through to the view on the other side of the river.

29

A royal river

Many of London's royal palaces and churches were built near the River Thames. This great river was once the main highway through the city, enabling kings and queens and their courtiers to travel quickly and smoothly from place to place.

HORSE GUARDS

Originally the site of the royal stables to Whitehall Palace.

ST. JAMES'S PALACE

Built by Henry VIII in 1536, today foreign ambassadors are still assigned to the Court of St. James.

KENSINGTON PALACE

Once a country retreat from the fumes of the city, today it's home to members of the Royal Family.

BUCKINGHAM PALACE

First occupied by Queen Victoria in 1837, this is the Queen's official home in London.

WESTMINSTER ABBEY

Kings and queens have been crowned here for a thousand years, although the present church dates from 1245.

ROYAL HOSPITAL CHELSEA

Home for retired soldiers, many of whom had fought in the Civil War, it was commissioned by Charles II and designed by Christopher Wren.

Hampton Court
this way

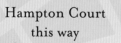

ST. PAUL'S CATHEDRAL

This magnificent church rises above the River Thames. Until modern skyscrapers, its huge dome dominated the London skyline.

TOWER OF LONDON

Officially still a royal palace, this Norman castle became a prison and place of execution for royal prisoners.

WHITEHALL

The Banqueting House is all that remains of the sprawling Palace of Whitehall, which was destroyed by fire in 1698.

PALACE OF WESTMINSTER

Once a royal palace, this is now the Houses of Parliament where politicians meet to pass laws.

ROYAL BARGES

Golden barges used to sail along the river carrying the Royal Family. A new barge was made for the Queen's Diamond Jubilee in 2012.

Greenwich this way

HAMPTON COURT

Lying to the west of London, this enormous brick and stone palace was built by Cardinal Wolsey and presented to Henry VIII.

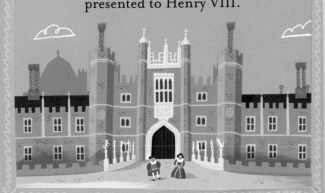

GREENWICH

The park surrounding Greenwich was once a hunting ground for kings and queens. At its heart is the Queen's House, one of the most beautiful buildings in the country.

Index

Usborne Quicklinks

For links to websites where you can zoom in on the Crown Jewels, see the Throne Room at Buckingham Palace, and discover more about people and places of royal London, go to the Usborne Quicklinks website at **www.usborne.com/quicklinks** and type in the title of this book. Please follow the internet safety guidelines at the Usborne Quicklinks website.

Acknowledgements

Cover: tl © The Print Collector/Alamy, tm © epa european pressphoto agency b.v./Alamy, ml © B Christopher/Alamy, br © Peter Phipp/Travelshots.com/Alamy; p2: tm © Andy Chopping/Museum of London Archaeology, ml © British Library Board. All Rights Reserved/Bridgeman Images, br © Joris van Ostaeyen/Alamy; p3: tl Private Collection/Bridgeman Images, mr © GL Archive/Alamy, bl © Peter Lane/Alamy; p4: tl © The Art Archive/Alamy, br © Peter Phipp/Travelshots.com/Alamy; p5: tl © The Art Archive/Alamy, mr © World History Archive/Alamy, br © Heritage Image Partnership Ltd/Alamy; p6: tl © Hulton-Deutsch Collection/Corbis, mr © World History Archive/Alamy, bl © GL Archive/Alamy, br © National Trust Photo Library/Alamy; p7: tm © epa european pressphoto agency b.v./Alamy, tr Holmes Garden Photos/Alamy, ml © The Print Collector/Alamy, mr © Michael Freeman/Alamy; p8: tm Private Collection/Bridgeman Images, tr Victoria & Albert Museum, London/Bridgeman Images, ml Musée de la Tapisserie/special authorisation city of Bayeux/Bridgeman Images; p9: tl © Bradford Art Galleries & Museums/Bridgeman Images, ml © Angelo Hornak/Alamy, mr © Rudy Sulgan/Corbis; p10: Royal Collection Trust © Her Majesty Queen Elizabeth II, 2014/Bridgeman Images, bl © Robert Preston/Alamy; p11: tl © Robert Harding Picture Library Ltd/Alamy, tm © V&A Images/Alamy, tr Private Collection/Stapleton Collection/Bridgeman Images, ml © The Art Archive/Alamy; p12: bl epa european pressphoto agency b.v./Alamy, bml © Hilary Morgan/Alamy, bmr © Alamy/Alamy, br © Suzanne Plunkett/Reuters/Corbis; p13: ml © Photography by Steve Allen/Alamy, mr © WENN UK/Alamy, bm © Nick Fielding/Alamy; p14: ml © Heritage Image Partnership Ltd/Alamy, mr © Eric Nathan/Alamy, bm © World History Archive/Alamy; p15: ml © Peter Barritt/Alamy, mm © Holmes Garden Photos/Alamy, mr © Homer Sykes/Alamy, br National Gallery of Art, Washington DC, USA/Bridgeman Images; p16: tr © Arthur Ackermann Ltd, London/Bridgeman Images, ml © Heritage Image Partnership Ltd/Alamy, br © Rolf Richardson/Alamy; p17: tr © Peter Barritt/Alamy, ml © Paul Thompson Images/Alamy, bl © David Cole/Alamy, mr Reproduced with permission of the Ministry of Defence; p18: ml © The Gallery Collection/Corbis, mr © Steve Vidler/Alamy, bm © Stu/Alamy; p19: tl © Stefano Ravera/Alamy, tm © Lebrecht Music and Art Photo Library/Alamy, mr Private Collection/Stapleton Collection/Bridgeman Images, bl The Grainger Collection/Topfoto; p20: tl © Angelo Hornak/Alamy, bm © Prisma Archivo/Alamy, br © Nigel J Clarke/Alamy; p21: tl World History Archive/Alamy, tr Brian Lawrence/Getty, ml © Angelo Hornak/Alamy, mm © Steve Vidler/Alamy, br © Martyn Goddard/Alamy; p22: tr © Philip Mould Ltd, London/Bridgeman Images, ml © Steve Vidler/Alamy, mr © Steve Vidler/Alamy, bl Harris Museum & Art Gallery, Preston, Lancashire/Bridgeman Images; p23: ml National Trust Photographic Library/John Hammond/Bridgeman Images, br © Jeff Gilbert/Alamy; p24: tl © World History Archive/Alamy, tm © English Heritage Photo Library/Bridgeman Images, mr Private Collection/Stapleton Collection/Bridgeman Images, bm © North Wind Picture Archives/Alamy; p25: tm Stuart Black/Getty, tr Royal Collection Trust © Her Majesty Queen Elizabeth II, 2014/Bridgeman Images, ml © WENN Ltd/Alamy, bl © Rex Features; p26: tr Hulton Archive/Stringer/Getty, bl © Justin Kase z10z/Alamy, br © Paul Brown/Alamy; p27: tr Royal Collection Trust © Her Majesty Queen Elizabeth II, 2014/Bridgeman Images, ml Royal Collection Trust © Her Majesty Queen Elizabeth II, 2014/Bridgeman Images, mr © Pictorial Press Ltd/Alamy, br © Terry Fincher.Photo Int/Alamy; p28: bl © Pawel Libera Images/Alamy, bm © Historic Royal Palaces; p29: tm © Gary Lucken/Alamy, mm © nik wheeler/Alamy, mr Travel Ink/Getty, br © jonathan tennant/Alamy

Edited by Jane Chisholm
Additional editor: Rachel Firth
Managing Designer: Nicola Butler
With thanks to Ruth King
Digital manipulation by John Russell & Brian Voakes